juice it

NH
NEW
HOLLAND

First published in 2008 by New Holland Publishers (UK) Ltd
London • Cape Town • Sydney • Auckland

Garfield House	80 McKenzie Street	66 Gibbes Street	218 Lake Road
86–88 Edgware Rd	Cape Town 8001	Chatswood	Northcote
London W2 2EA	South Africa	NSW 2067	Auckland
United Kingdom		Australia	New Zealand

ISBN 978 1 84773 232 3

Senior Editor Corinne Masciocchi
Designer Lucy Parissi
Photographer Ian Garlick
Food stylist Wendy Sweetser
Production Marion Storz
Editorial Direction Rosemary Wilkinson

1 3 5 7 9 10 8 6 4 2

Reproduction by Pica Digital Pte Ltd, Singapore
Printed and bound by Tien Wah Press (Pte) Ltd, Malaysia

The recipes in this book were tested using a Breville JE4 Commercial Juicer and a Breville AWT Professional Juicer.

As a rough guideline, 250 ml (9 fl oz) makes enough juice to fill one medium-size tumbler.

juice it

wendy sweetser

contents

introduction   6

energy boosters   14

super soothers   44

instant revivers   72

liquid snacks on the go   100

let's celebrate   128

time to detox   158

index   190

introduction

There's nothing quite like a freshly squeezed juice you've made yourself. Pour it into a long, cool glass and before you've even taken the first mouthful you just know it's going to make you feel good.

The big advantage of homemade juices over bought ones is that you get to decide what goes into them. You can sharpen their flavour by adding more citrus, sweeten them by dropping in a few extra strawberries or a larger slice of melon and when you feel you need a beetroot or cabbage detox but can't face too much of their earthy taste, you can disguise them with more palatable ingredients like carrots and apples.

As about 95% of the nutrients in fruit and vegetables are found in their juice, the liquid extracted from them forms an important part of a balanced diet, so making juices is an easy and highly enjoyable way of upping your intake of body-boosting minerals and vitamins.

Even though, strictly speaking, however many different fruits and vegetables you juice together they only count as one portion of your recommended daily allowance of five a day in the finished glassful, homemade juices are fresher and therefore better for you than any standard commercially-made variety. Also, opening a carton of bought juice just doesn't compare with the good feeling you get when you pour a glass of juice you've made yourself!

dragon fruit

wheatgrass

root ginger

pomegranate

Which kind of juicer should I buy?

There is a wide variety of juicers on the market, from basic machines to the expensive heavy-duty pulverizers used by sandwich shops and juice bars.

The simplest and cheapest juicer of all is an old-fashioned lemon squeezer or citrus press. If you only want to make orange juice or need lemon juice to add to a drink, this will extract more juice from a citrus fruit than any other machine.

Most juicers you'll find on sale are the type known as 'centrifugal extractors' where fruit and vegetables are pushed down a feeder tube into a spinning basket with a grater in the base. The pulp is shredded and trapped whilst the juice shoots out the side and into a jug.

The more expensive the machine, the bigger its motor will be, so more juice is extracted and it is better equipped to cope with fibrous fruit and vegetables. Less powerful juicers may have an automatic 'cut-out' that kicks in when the machine is put under excess stress from too many tough ingredients being pushed down the feeder tube at once, but when juicing fibrous ingredients like pumpkin, Brussels sprouts or beetroot in any kind of machine it helps to cut them into small pieces first.

When buying a juicer, always follow the manufacturer's safety instructions carefully when assembling, using and dismantling the machine.

centrifugal extractor

borage flowers

Is any other equipment needed to make juices?
A blender is useful as bananas make such a great addition to
so many blended drinks but are impossible to juice. To get the
maximum nutritional benefits from a banana it's better to liquidize
it in a blender with the finished juice rather than feed it through
the juicer and watch it disappear immediately into the pulp.

A blender can also be used to make many of the fruit drinks in
this book but the fruit has to be peeled first and any pips, cores
and seeds removed. As both the pulp and the juice are blended,
the resulting drink will be a smoothie and therefore thicker. If it's
too thick, dilute it down with mineral water or extra fruit juice.

What should I look for when buying ingredients for juicing?
Avoid buying over-ripe fruit or vegetables for juicing that are
past their best as their nutrients and juice content diminish with
age. All ingredients should be ripe but firm and fruit should
smell sweet and fragrant.

If the produce you want to use is out of season, frozen can be
substituted as long as it has been frozen immediately after picking
to preserve its nutrients. Tinned fruit and vegetables lose many of

their nutrients during the canning process so are best avoided unless you want to include a fruit with a particularly distinctive flavour, such as lychees or mango, in a party drink.

How do I prepare ingredients for juicing?

As many of the nutrients in fruit and vegetables are found just under the skin, it follows you'll get a healthier juice if you leave the skin on. All produce – whether organic or non-organic – must be washed thoroughly first in warm water but only remove the skin if it is very hard. For instance, a watermelon has thin, smooth skin that contains lots of juice so it can be left on, whereas a Galia melon has a tough, dry skin that is likely to jam a juicer if it's not cut away.

Remove any tough stalks and hard stones from fruits like plums or apricots, but apple cores, melon seeds and celery leaves can all be left in.

Citrus fruits should always be peeled, unless being squeezed in a citrus press, as their rind will give a drink a bitter taste if it's put through a juicer. The pith contains valuable nutrients so only cut away the thin outer zest using a vegetable peeler.

Before juicing, cut prepared fruit and vegetables into slices or chunks small enough for them to fit comfortably down the feeder tube of the juicer. Each of the recipes in this book gives details on how to prepare the ingredients used.

Do I need to sweeten juices?

This depends on individual taste but generally it's not necessary as most juices, whether fruit or vegetable ones, tend to be sweeter than the individual ingredients used to make it. Taste the finished juice first and if you feel it needs it, sweeten with sugar syrup, runny honey, caster sugar or a low-calorie sweetener.

How do I clean a juicer?

This is the boring bit as cleaning any kind of juicer is a chore. Discarded pulp is messy and you have to dismantle the machine and wash each part thoroughly every time you use it.

wild blackberries

Before buying a juicer, check how simple it is to put together and take apart and how easy the components are to clean. If your juicer has a separate pulp collector that can be lined with a freezer bag, the washing up will be less and the debris can go straight into your compost maker.

A small brush (often provided with the juicer) is needed to shift any pulp stuck in the grinder as any residue left in the machine will encourage harmful bacteria to grow.

How long will juices keep?
Juices are best drunk freshly made as the longer they're stored the more vitamins will be lost as they start to oxidize when they are exposed to the air. This oxidation process also causes juices containing apples and bananas to discolour and although this can be slowed down by the addition of lemon juice, it's still better to drink the juice when it's freshly made.

If making larger quantities of juices for a party, prepare them ahead as near to the party start time as practicable and store in the fridge or a cool place until needed.

If juices are made ahead and separate, give them a good stir before pouring into glasses. They can also be served with 'swizzle sticks' of melon, pepper or celery for drinkers to stir up themselves.

Some juices also thicken up on standing so let them down to the desired consistency with mineral water or extra fruit juice just before serving.

How can I get rid of too much froth on a juice?

Some fruits, such as apples, make a lot of froth when juiced and as fruity 'cappuccinos' are not to everyone's taste. The froth can be removed or reduced in several ways.

The juice-collecting jugs that are supplied with some machines come with a built-in froth separator in the shape of a lid that traps the froth in the jug as you pour off the juice into a glass. If your machine doesn't have such a jug, the quickest way to remove froth is to skim it off with a spoon.

You also can reduce the amount of froth produced by passing hard fruits and vegetables through the juicer after softer ones have been juiced and spraying a mist of cold water over a juice to help the froth settle.

However, there is no reason why the froth can't be drunk, so leave it in a foaming layer on top or stir it into the juice if you prefer.

Are there any special juicing tips I should know?

If your juicer has two speeds and the fruit and vegetables are of different textures, juice the softer ones first on low speed and then increase to high speed for harder ingredients.

When juicing herbs, Brussels sprouts or leafy vegetables like spinach or cabbage, juice them in the middle of other ingredients on low speed to extract the maximum amount of juice.

When adding fruit and vegetables to the juicer, push the pieces down the feeder tube with the food pusher – never your hands – to extract the most juice. If you cannot process all the ingredients in one go, switch the machine off and let the mechanism slow down and stop before you lift the food pusher to add the remainder.

Can I juice any combination of fruit and vegetables?

strawberries

A juice needs to look fresh and inviting so whilst, in theory, you can juice any combination of ingredients you feel like, try to picture what the final colour will be as a glass that resembles pond water or liquid mud is unlikely to tempt your taste buds!

It's also worth avoiding mixing too many strong flavours as they'll fight each other for domination in the finished juice. Even just one very strong flavour – which will increase in strength if the juice is left to stand – can overpower more subtle flavours that you want to come through.

As some fruit and vegetables contain more juice than others it is a good idea to combine denser ingredients with those that have a high moisture content to achieve an acceptable yield.

NOTES ON THE RECIPES IN THIS BOOK

 Quantities given for the individual juices are only approximate as these will vary according to the size of fruit and vegetables, how much moisture they contain and the type of juicing machine used.

 Although juices are good for you, fun to make and even better to drink, the recipes in this book are intended to be enjoyed as part of a healthy balanced diet, not as a way to turn a junk food diet into a healthy one or as any kind of weight loss regime.

ENERGY
BOOSTERS

breakfast smoothie

Oranges are a well known source of vitamin C but what's less well known is that kiwi fruit contain twice as much of the precious vitamin, plus more fibre than apples. All three fruits, along with potassium-rich bananas, combine to make this power-packed breakfast drink the perfect start to any day. If time is short, you may prefer to make this as a traditional smoothie by blending the banana and kiwi fruit in a blender with 1 orange (peeled, segmented and pips removed) and 150 ml (5 fl oz) each of orange juice and apple juice.

Makes 500 ml (18 fl oz)

1 banana

1 large orange

1 kiwi fruit

3 apples

Method

Peel the banana and cut into three or four pieces. Cut the rind off the orange using a vegetable peeler but leaving the pith attached to the fruit, and cut into chunks. Peel the kiwi fruit. Twist the stalks off the apples and cut into quarters.

Juice the orange, kiwi fruit and apples, pour into a blender, add the banana and liquidize. Pour into glasses and serve.

bright eyes

Don't dismiss parsley as just a frilly garnish to be moved to the side of your dinner plate and ignored, as this favourite herb not only aids digestion, it also acts as an effective diuretic. Juiced with the refreshing combination of carrot, orange and apple, it's a great way to kick-start your day, especially if you suffer the miseries of bloating caused by water retention.

Makes 500 ml (18 fl oz)
225 g (8 oz) carrots
1 apple
2 oranges
2 Tbsp chopped fresh parsley

Method

Top, tail and chop the carrots. Twist the stalk off the apple and cut into quarters. Cut the rind off the oranges using a vegetable peeler.

Juice the carrots, apple and oranges, pour into glasses and sprinkle the parsley on top.

citrus blitz

Pick up an orange grown in Florida and it will feel heavier than one from Jaffa or Spain as the Sunshine State's mix of bright sun and sudden downpours gives its oranges a thinner rind and extra juice. All citrus fruits are rich in vitamin C so this juice is a good way of achieving your recommended daily amount of 60 mg a day.

Makes 500 ml (18 fl oz)

1 grapefruit

3 large oranges

1 lime, plus extra to garnish

Ice cubes

Method
Shave the rind off the grapefruit, oranges and lime using a vegetable peeler, leaving on the pith. Cut the fruit into wedges or chunks, and juice.

Serve chilled or poured over ice garnished with extra lime slices or wedges.

four all

Nectarines are a fuzz-free cousin of the peach rather than, as many believe, a cross between a peach and a plum, and these sweet, juicy fruit have been grown in China for more than 2,000 years. They arrived in the UK around the end of the 16th century and Spanish explorers introduced them to America where today California is one of the nectarine-growing capitals of the world. Either white or yellow-fleshed nectarines can be used to make this drink.

Makes 600 ml (1 pt)
2 apples
2 pears
2 nectarines
175 g (6 oz) strawberries

Method
Twist the stalks off the apples and pears and cut each fruit into quarters. Halve the nectarines and remove the stones. There's no need to hull the strawberries if you are putting them through a juicer.

Juice the fruits together and pour into glasses.

fruit-full

The golden germ in a grain of wheat might only be tiny but it is a concentrated food, so adding wheat germ to a juice is an easy way to raise its nutritional profile. Not that this juice's profile needs any raising, as with potassium from bananas, vitamin C from cranberries and strawberries, and antioxidants from blueberries and apples, it's an A-lister in its own right but, as they say, a little extra always helps!

Makes 200 ml (7 fl oz)

1 banana

1 apple

115 g (4 oz) strawberries, plus extra to garnish

50 g (2 oz) blueberries, plus extra to garnish

50 g (2 oz) frozen cranberries, thawed

2 Tbsp wheat germ

Method

Peel the banana and cut into three or four pieces. Twist the stalk off the apple and cut into quarters. Leave the strawberries whole.

Juice the apple, strawberries, blueberries and cranberries together with half the wheat germ. Pour the juice into a blender, add the banana and whiz until smooth.

Pour into glasses, sprinkle with the remaining wheat germ and serve decorated with extra strawberries and blueberries.

guava buzz

Guavas first grew in Central America and the Caribbean Islands and from there they migrated to tropical countries around the world. The fruit can be eaten both ripe and when it is still green, although ripe guavas that are fragrant and sweet are obviously better for juicing. Crunchy unripe slices are a favourite snack in Thailand, where the locals enjoy them dipped in sugar or salt.

Makes 300 ml (½ pt)

6 guavas

10 apricots

2 pears

Crushed ice

Method

Halve the guavas. Halve the apricots and remove the stones. Twist the stalks off the pears and cut into quarters. Juice all the fruits together.

Serve poured into glasses over crushed ice.

just peachy

Hailed by modern scientists as a superfood packed with antioxidants that protect the body from free radicals or 'bad' chemicals in the blood, pomegranates have now moved centre stage after languishing for centuries in the culinary wilderness. This leathery-skinned fruit has been around since the dawn of history and Persian historians believe it was a pomegranate rather than an apple that tempted Eve in the Garden of Eden. In this juice, the red crunchy seeds provide a satisfying contrast to the sweet mandarin and peach juices. If you buy a pack of pomegranate seeds rather than a whole fruit, use 2 tablespoons of seeds.

Makes 500 ml (18 fl oz)

4 mandarins
2 yellow flesh peaches
Seeds of 1 pomegranate
Borage flowers,
to garnish (optional)

Method
Peel the mandarins. Halve the peaches and remove the stones. Cut the pomegranate in half across the centre and pop out the seeds with a skewer or the point of a knife.

Juice the mandarins and peaches, pour into glasses and drop in the pomegranate seeds. Float a few borage flowers on top of each serving for a pretty final flourish.

morning glory

Plums vary enormously in colour and flavour, ranging from pale green to deep purple and from tart to very sweet. Like most soft fruit, plums are best eaten fresh in season but if you have plum trees in your garden and a bumper crop, any excess fruit can be frozen and used for juicing and in cooked dishes like crumbles and pies. Pomelo gives this juice a tart flavour so if you find it too sharp for your taste, add a little honey or sugar syrup to sweeten.

Makes 500 ml (18 fl oz)

1 pomelo

225 g (8 oz) red-skinned plums

200 g (7 oz) raspberries, plus extra to garnish

Method

Cut the rind off the pomelo using a vegetable peeler and cut the flesh (with the pith still attached) into chunks. Halve the plums and remove the stones and stalks.

Juice the fruits, pour into glasses and garnish with a few extra raspberries.

power punch

It might not give you the muscles of Popeye, but spinach is very definitely a body builder. Overflowing with vitamin C, iron and beta-carotene, the rich green leaves contain oxygen-boosting chlorophyll, are a good source of fibre, and boost the circulation system. However, spinach is also high in oxalic acid, which if taken in large quantities, affects the body's ability to absorb calcium, so the leaves need to be mixed with other fruit and vegetables rather than juiced on their own.

Makes 350 ml (12 fl oz)

115 g (4 oz) spinach leaves

1 apple

½ cucumber, plus extra to garnish

1 kiwi fruit

Method

Coarsely shred the spinach leaves if large. Twist the stalk off the apple and cut into quarters. Chop the cucumber into chunks and peel the kiwi fruit.

Juice the spinach, apple, cucumber and kiwi fruit, pour into glasses and garnish with strips of cucumber.

purple haze

The wrinklier the skin, the juicier a passion fruit so don't be put off by fruit that looks worn out and past its best. Make this juice using either Ogen or Galia melon: the Galia is a relative of the Ogen but as it has a rough, dry skin cut this away before juicing the flesh. Ogen, like watermelon, has a softer skin so it doesn't need peeling before juicing. The seeds can be blitzed in as well to increase the vitamin E and zinc content of the juice.

Makes 300 ml (½ pt)

½ Ogen or Galia melon, about 400 g (14 oz), plus extra to garnish

1 passion fruit

115 g (4 oz) blueberries

175 g (6 oz) blackberries

Method

If using Ogen melon, leave it unpeeled, if using Galia, cut away the skin. Cut the melon into chunks, setting aside a few extra slices for decoration. Halve and scoop the pulp and seeds out of the passion fruit.

Juice all the fruits together, including the passion fruit seeds, pour into glasses and serve with the melon slices to garnish.

red alert

Homemade tomato juice is not as thick and concentrated as the shop-bought variety so is more refreshing, especially when mixed with a sweet-flavoured vegetable such as carrot. The first tomatoes grew wild along South America's winding west coast but they are now cultivated around the world. Rich in antioxidants, particularly carotenoids such as beta-carotene and lycopene, and vitamins A and E, they are an important player in a healthy diet, helping to protect against heart disease and some cancers.

Makes 500 ml (18 fl oz)

750 g (1 lb 10 oz) ripe tomatoes

85 g (3 oz) carrots

1 celery stick with leaves

Extra carrot or celery sticks, to serve

Method

Halve the tomatoes. Top, tail and chop the carrots into chunks. Cut the celery into 5 cm (2 in) lengths.

Juice the vegetables and pour into glasses. Garnish with a celery or carrot stick as the juice separates quite quickly and this can be used to give it a good stir before drinking.

rosy glow

Squeezing citrus fruits using an old-fashioned lemon press extracts the most juice from the fruit but because the pith stays behind you lose the powerful antioxidants it contains called bioflavonoids. As these bioflavonoids work with vitamin C, something all citrus fruit are packed with, it's worth juicing the pith along with the flesh. Grapefruit are naturally sharp but their sweetness increases with their colour so the pinker the grapefruit the sweeter it will be.

Makes 500 ml (18 fl oz)

1 papaya, weighing about 600 g (1 lb 5 oz)

½ grapefruit

150 g (5½ oz) strawberries, plus extra to garnish

A few mint leaves, to garnish

Method

Halve the papaya and scoop out the seeds. Cut away the rind from the grapefruit using a vegetable peeler, leaving the pith attached to the flesh. Leave the strawberries whole – there's no need to hull them.

Juice the fruits, pour into glasses and serve garnished with strawberry slices and mint leaves.

start right

If a poll were held to find the world's most fragrant fruit, passion fruit would surely romp home. At first glance, the wrinkled, purple, ping pong balls don't look very exciting but cut one in half and the scent of the seedy pulp inside is positively seductive. The seeds can be juiced with the pulp but as they have a pleasantly crunchy texture it's nice to just stir them into the finished drink. However, as the pulp tends to make them clump together, warm the seeds and pulp first to separate the two. Golden or ordinary kiwi fruit work equally well if the red heart variety are not available.

Makes 500 ml (18 fl oz)

2 passion fruit

3 oranges

2 red heart kiwi fruit, plus extra to garnish

Method

Cut the passion fruit in half, scoop out the pulp and seeds into a cup or bowl and warm in the microwave or in a small pan on the hob until the seeds separate from the pulp. Leave to cool.

Cut the rind from the oranges using a vegetable peeler and chop the fruit into chunks. Peel the kiwi fruit.

Juice the oranges and kiwi fruit and stir in the passion fruit pulp and seeds. Pour into glasses and serve garnished with extra kiwi slices.

up-beet

Beetroot gives juices a real health boost as it's full of minerals and vitamins that cleanse the blood and help fight fatigue after an exhausting day. Try partnering it with sweeter tasting produce, such as apples or carrots to balance its strong flavour. Beetroot will also give a juice a gorgeous, jewel-like hue but, be warned, if you drink a lot the colour will pass straight through you so don't panic when you go to the loo! Use well-scrubbed raw beetroot and cut it into small pieces so its fibrous texture passes more easily through the jaws of the juicer.

Makes 200 ml (7 fl oz)

225 g (8 oz) carrots

1 medium beetroot

115 g (4oz) watercress

1 cm (⅜ in) piece of root ginger

Method

Top, tail and chop the carrots, cut the beetroot into small wedges (reserving any small leaves for garnish) and discard any yellow watercress leaves. Thinly slice the ginger, leaving the skin on unless it is shrivelled.

Juice the vegetables and ginger and pour into small glasses. Serve garnished with any reserved beetroot leaves.

SUPER
SOOTHERS

berry nice

Until the early 17th century all the strawberries grown in Europe were of the tiny, wild, Alpine variety. They were eaten both for pleasure and medicinal purposes as strawberries help purge the body of uric acid and thus brought relief to millions of gourmets who suffered with painful joints. The large succulent berries we're more used to today are all descended from two American varieties and, as well as helping ease pain in the joints, strawberries contain high levels of vitamin C and soluble fibre to break down cholesterol. When juicing strawberries don't bother to remove the hulls, just add the whole fruit, stalk and all.

Makes 300 ml (½ pt)
115 g (4 oz) strawberries
115 g (4 oz) raspberries
115 g (4 oz) blackberries
115 g (4 oz) blueberries
A few extra berries,
to garnish

Method
Juice all the berries together. Pour into glasses and serve garnished with extra fruits.

chill out

Although not in the super-league when judged on the nutrient levels they contain, pears are still a good source of soluble fibre, vitamin C and potassium. They also add their own special fragrance to a juice drink and you will find that slightly under-ripe pears give better juicing results than fully-ripe fruit. Any variety of pear works well, from the modest Conference or Comice to their more luscious Williams cousin.

Makes 300 ml (½ pt)

115 g (4 oz) spinach leaves

2 pears

50 g (2 oz) watercress, plus extra sprigs to garnish

Method

Coarsely chop any large spinach leaves. Twist the stalks off the pears and cut the fruit into quarters. Discard any yellow watercress leaves.

Juice the spinach, pears and watercress and pour into glasses. Serve garnished with small watercress sprigs.

golden glow

An ancient Himalayan tribe called the Hunzas first prized apricots for their health benefits. Hunza apricots are still grown in Kashmir's Hunza valley and across Asia, but few would recognize the small, hard, beige-coloured fruit that has to be soaked and cooked before it can be eaten, as the plump orange fruit we're familiar with. Because the flesh of apricots is quite dry, they either need juicing with fruits such as oranges, or can be puréed and diluted to the desired consistency.

Makes 700 ml (1¼ pt)
4 apricots
1 medium mango
2 peaches
2 large oranges
Shredded orange zest,
to garnish

Juicing method
Halve and stone the apricots. Cut the unpeeled flesh of the mango away from the stone. Halve, stone and slice the peaches thickly. Cut the rind away from the oranges, and cut into chunks. Juice all the fruit and pour into glasses.

Blender method
Prepare the apricots and peaches in the same way but peel the mango. Peel and segment the oranges, removing all the pith and any seeds. Liquidize all the fruit in a blender and dilute to the desired consistency with mineral water or extra orange juice.

Serve garnished with shreds of orange zest.

green light

Taking grapes to a friend in hospital might seem a bit of a cliché but grapes contain so many good things they should be prescribed free! Rich in powerful antioxidants, they protect against heart disease and cancers and help overcome a variety of conditions from anaemia and arthritis to lowering blood pressure and speeding up recovery after serious illness or an operation. Red grapes are richer in antioxidants but both are highly nutritious when made into drinks.

Makes 400 ml (14 fl oz)

2 kiwi fruit

175 g (6 oz) seedless green or red grapes

2 apples

1 pomegranate or 2 Tbsp pomegranate seeds

Ice cubes

Method
Peel the kiwi fruit and de-stalk the grapes. Twist the stalk off the apples and cut into quarters. Juice the fruits. If using a whole pomegranate, cut in half and pop out the seeds.

Pour into glasses over ice and sprinkle in the pomegranate seeds.

in the mood

If Adam and Eve used fig leaves to preserve their modesty, presumably figs were regularly on the menu in the Garden of Eden. As with so many ancient fruits, figs are part medicine/part sheer indulgence, being a valuable source of fibre, iron and potassium but also acknowledged throughout Asia as one of nature's great aphrodisiacs.

Makes 500 ml (18 fl oz)
½ cantaloupe melon
1 large orange
1 banana
2 figs

Method
Cut the unpeeled melon into chunks small enough to fit down the feeder tube of the juicer. Cut the rind away from the orange using a vegetable peeler, leaving the pith attached to the flesh. Slice or cut into chunks. Peel and cut the banana into three or four pieces.

Juice the melon and orange with one fig. Pour into a blender, add the banana and liquidize until smooth.

Pour into glasses, cut the remaining fig into slices and use to garnish the drinks.

just relax

Cucumber and celery are two of nature's natural diuretics and make refreshingly soothing juices, especially when the sweetness of carrot and pineapple is added to the blend. Juice cucumber and celery that is firm and crisp, rather than limp sticks that are drying out and past their sell-by date.

Makes 350 ml (12 fl oz)

½ cucumber

100 g (3½ oz) carrots

1 celery stick with leaves

½ small pineapple, about 400 g (14 oz) unpeeled weight

Celery sticks and pineapple leaves, to garnish

Method

Cut the cucumber into chunks. Top, tail and chop the carrots. Coarsely chop the celery and leaves. Peel the pineapple and cut into chunks.

Juice the vegetables and pineapple, pour into glasses and serve garnished with celery sticks and pineapple leaves.

melon breeze

Stir extra lemon juice into the finished drink if you prefer it to have a sharper taste or if you've been lucky enough to find melons that are really sweet and fragrant and find the extra sweetness needs balancing with a citrus edge. This juice is especially good served chilled on a warm summer's day.

Makes 500 ml (18 fl oz)

½ Ogen or cantaloupe melon

½ mini watermelon, weighing about 675 g (1 lb 8 oz)

1 small lemon or ½ large lemon

Ice cubes (optional)

Shredded mint leaves, to garnish

Method

Cut the melons into chunks without removing the peel or the seeds. Peel the lemon, leaving on the pith, and remove the seeds.

Juice all the fruit together, reserving a few small pieces of watermelon for garnish, and adjusting the flavour by adding extra lemon juice if preferred. Pour into chilled glasses or serve over ice. Garnish with the reserved watermelon and sprinkle with a little finely shredded mint.

night cap

The perfect way to wind down after a long and trying day, particularly when the winter sniffles are getting you down. Prepare the basic juice mix ahead, then pour into heatproof glasses or mugs and top up with hot water when you are ready to put your feet up and relax.

Makes 600 ml (1 pt) when topped up with hot water

2 apples

1 lemon

1 orange

Small piece of cinnamon stick

Hot water

1–2 tsp clear honey, or to taste

Extra orange wedges and apple slices, to garnish

Method

Twist the stalks off the apples and cut the fruit into quarters. Shave the rind off the lemon and orange and roughly chop the flesh. Juice all the fruit and chill until needed.

When ready to serve, half fill a glass or mug with juice, add a small piece of cinnamon stick and top up with hot water. Stir in clear honey to taste. Serve garnished with orange wedges and apple slices and remove the cinnamon stick before drinking.

no stress

Sweet potatoes are rich in vitamin C and vitamin E and they make a really good – if unlikely – addition to juices. No relation to ordinary potatoes, their sweet, red-orange flesh is higher in fibre than normal potatoes and contains lots of beta-carotene to boost the immune system. Columbus first brought sweet potatoes back to Europe from where they found their way to Britain and soon became the latest must-have food. Just as quickly their popularity waned and they didn't reappear on greengrocers' stalls until the 1950s and 60s when people from the Caribbean islands began migrating to Britain and longed for a taste of home. Parsnip makes this juice quite creamy so increase the amount of cabbage if you prefer a sharper taste.

Makes 200 ml (7 fl oz)
175 g (6 oz) green
cabbage leaves
225 g (8 oz) parsnips
1 small sweet potato
Ice cubes (optional)

Method
Shred the cabbage leaves or cut into pieces that will fit easily down the feeder tube of the juicer. Cut the parsnips and sweet potato to fit as well – neither needs peeling.

Juice all the vegetables and pour into chilled glasses or serve over ice.

pink panther

Each May the people of Northern Thailand celebrate the start of the new lychee season with village festivals and plenty of partying. These creamy, grape-like berries with their rough skins and shiny brown seeds are looked on as a food of love, with suitors giving them as a special gift to their sweetheart, often with the hint of a proposal to follow. A good source of vitamin C, lychees also contain potassium to help cells, nerves and blood pressure function as they should.

Makes 400 ml (14 fl oz)

700 g (1 lb 9 oz) wedge of honeydew melon

8 lychees

175 g (6 oz) strawberries

125 g (4½ oz) raspberries

Method

Cut the unpeeled melon into chunks without removing the seeds. Peel the lychees and remove the seeds. Cut any large strawberries in half – there's no need to hull them.

Juice the melon, lychees, strawberries and raspberries. Pour into glasses and serve.

red mist

If you're new to juicing, don't cringe at the thought of tossing your least favourite vegetables like cabbage or Brussels sprouts down the feeder tube as, while it's true most vegetable juices (apart from carrot) are too strong to drink neat, if you mix them with sweeter ingredients they become deliciously palatable. As carrots are high in fibre and cabbage aids digestion this juice really hits the spot if you've over-indulged on all the wrong things.

Makes 400 ml (14 fl oz)

150 g (5½ oz) red cabbage, plus a little extra to garnish

1 large pear

225 g (8 oz) carrots, plus a little extra to garnish

Method

Discard any discoloured outer leaves from the cabbage and cut away any tough stalk or core. Shred or cut the cabbage into wedges small enough to fit down the feeder tube of the juicer. Twist the stalk off the pear and cut into quarters or wedges. Top and tail the carrots and cut into chunks.

Juice the cabbage, pear and carrots and pour into glasses. Garnish with whisker-thin shreds of cabbage and a little grated carrot.

summer special

This iced lemon and mint tea makes a refreshingly cool drink on a warm day. The tea can be made in a pot or a heatproof jug, then left to brew to the required strength before being poured into glasses or cups. China tea has a more delicate flavour than Indian, making it a better foil for the lemon and fresh mint. Sweeten the tea according to personal taste.

Makes about 600 ml (1 pt) depending on the amount of crushed ice used

1 large lemon

2 China tea bags (eg Keemun or Lapsang souchong)

450 ml (16 fl oz) boiling water

Sugar, to taste

Crushed ice

4 mint sprigs, to serve

Extra lemon slices, to serve

Method

Halve and squeeze the juice from the lemon. Put the tea bags into a warmed teapot or heatproof jug and pour over the boiling water. Stir in the lemon juice and sugar to taste.

Leave to brew for 5 minutes before removing the tea bags and pouring the tea into four heatproof glasses half-filled with crushed ice. Add mint sprigs and extra lemon slices to each glass and drink when cool.

tropical teaser

If you're a fitness freak, pineapple should be top of your shopping list as its sweet fibrous flesh contains bromelain, a natural enzyme that works hard at repairing strained muscles and sprained joints and reducing the effects of bruising. It's important to buy a pineapple that is ripe as under-ripe fruit are sharp, chewy and lack the all-important healing benefits. Once a pineapple is harvested it won't ripen further, so choose one that feels heavy for its size and has a fragrant, sweet scent.

Makes 600 ml (1 pt)

1 medium papaya

1 pineapple, weighing about 700 g (1 lb 9 oz)

2 passion fruit

Method

Cut the papaya in half, scoop out and discard the seeds. Cut the unpeeled flesh into chunks. Trim the leaves off the pineapple and cut away the skin, removing the 'eyes'. Quarter the pineapple, cut out the tough centre core and chop the flesh into chunks. Juice the papaya and pineapple.

Cut the passion fruit in half, scoop out the pulp and seeds into a small bowl and warm gently to separate the two. Cool before whisking into the juice. If preferred, the pulp can be put through the juicer with the papaya and pineapple to remove the seeds.

INSTANT
REVIVERS

agent orange

For dieters, celery is a 'negative' food as it contains only seven calories per 100 g (3½ oz) and you burn more calories chewing and digesting it than you consume, but if you're making a juice, celery is deliciously soothing and cleansing, and its slight saltiness helps take the edge off sweeter flavours. The greener the leaves and stems the more beta-carotene and folic acid they will contain but the stems must be crisp so avoid any that are limp and floppy.

Makes 600 ml (1 pt)

½ papaya, weighing about 300 g (10½ oz)

3 large oranges, plus extra wedges to serve

2 celery sticks with leaves, plus extra leaves to garnish

Method

Scoop the seeds out of the papaya and chop the unpeeled flesh. Cut the rind away from the oranges, leaving the pith attached to the flesh, and chop. Cut the celery into short lengths.

Juice the papaya, oranges and celery and pour into glasses. Garnish with orange wedges and celery leaves and serve.

apricot and orange spritz

When apricots are out of season this cordial could be made using dried ones but it's worth simmering them first for 10 minutes in a pan of water so they plump up and soften, making them easier to purée. Make the purée ahead and keep it refrigerated until needed.

Makes 850 ml (1½ pt) when topped up with sparkling mineral water

300 g (10½ oz) apricots

3 large oranges

½ lemon

Ice cubes

450 ml (16 fl oz) soda water

Method

Halve and stone the apricots.
Peel and segment the oranges and squeeze the juice from the lemon. Put the apricots, oranges and lemon juice in a blender and whiz until smooth. Pour into a jug and chill until needed.

Put four or five ice cubes in each glass and half fill the glasses with the fruit purée. Top up with sparkling mineral water or soda water and serve at once.

back to your roots

In the Middle Ages, doctors believed parsnips were a panacea for all kinds of ills from easing toothache and stomach upsets to increasing male potency and even warding off adders. Today we're more circumspect and often dismiss the humble parsnip as just a dull winter vegetable but this pale relative of the carrot really deserves better. Not only does it add sweetness to a juice, it also contains a healthy mix of vitamins and minerals that are good for shiny hair, strong nails and clearer skin. When adding the vegetables to the juicer, don't over-pack the feeder tube as sweet potato, carrot and parsnip are all dense-textured and if they are too tightly packed, the pieces will jam and not pass through easily.

Makes 300 ml (½ pt)
1 medium sweet potato
2 medium carrots
1 medium parsnip
¼ cucumber
2 Tbsp snipped fresh chives

Method
Chop the unpeeled sweet potato. Top and tail the carrots and cut into chunks. Trim the top of the parsnip and cut into thick slices. Cut the cucumber into short lengths.

Juice the sweet potato, carrots, parsnip and cucumber and pour into glasses. Sprinkle with the snipped chives and serve.

blue moon

Their deep purple berries might look small and unassuming but the humble blueberry is a powerhouse in the good health stakes. Laden with antioxidants to boost our immune system and fight disease, blueberries also help overcome bladder problems like cystitis, protect eyes by reducing the risk of cataracts and keep blood flowing smoothly through our veins. One of these antioxidants – flavenoids – is also a collagen booster that helps keep skin more elastic and younger looking for longer. And that has to be good news!

Makes 600 ml (1 pt)

850 g (1 lb 14 oz) honeydew melon

200 g (7 oz) blueberries

150 g (5½ oz) blackberries

Lemon juice (optional)

Method

Cut the unpeeled melon into chunks, leaving the seeds in. Juice with the blueberries and blackberries and taste for sweetness. If necessary, add a little lemon juice to sharpen the flavour. Pour into glasses and serve.

chill out lemon

This sharp, tangy lemonade is made by simply whizzing whole lemons in a blender and then straining the pulpy juice into glasses before topping up with cold water. Drunk on its own the lemonade is very tart so it needs sweetening by adding sugar to taste and a couple of scoops of lemon sorbet – a delicious way to keep cool on a hot day.

Makes about 500 ml (18 fl oz) when topped up with still water

2 whole large lemons

2–3 Tbsp caster sugar, or to taste

Still mineral or tap water

4 large or 8 small scoops of lemon sorbet

Method

Cut the lemons into chunks and place in a blender with 2 tablespoons caster sugar. Blend until smooth. Strain into a measuring jug, pushing as much of the pulp as you can through the strainer with a wooden spoon. Taste the juice and add more sugar to taste, although remember the lemon sorbet will also sweeten it. Top up to 500 ml (18 fl oz) with still water.

Pour into tumblers and add one or two scoops of lemon sorbet to each. Allow the sorbet to melt a little before drinking.

fine and dandy

Dandelion leaves have been used for centuries as a diuretic, something that's not lost on the French where they are sold piled on village market stalls as salad leaves and called 'pissenlit' (wet the bed). The slightly bitter leaves are rich in iron and vitamins A and C so if you have dandelions growing in your garden, don't just pull them up, add a handful of the young leaves to a juice, balancing their bitter flavour with sweeter vegetables like peppers or carrots.

Makes 200 ml (7 fl oz)

150 g (5½ oz) fennel bulb

1 yellow pepper

115 g (4 oz) spinach leaves

15 g (½ oz) young dandelion leaves, plus a few extra to garnish

Method

Slice the fennel bulb and the pepper without discarding the stalk and seeds. Shred any large spinach leaves.

Juice the fennel, pepper, spinach and dandelion leaves and pour into glasses. Garnish with a few extra dandelion leaves and serve.

ginger fizz

Since the dawn of time apples have been one of nature's superfoods. Two apples a day are said to lower cholesterol and the malic and tartaric acids found in apples aid digestion by breaking down fat, hence the wisdom of serving apple sauce with roast pork or sage and apple stuffing with duck and goose. The best apples for juicing are crisp, tart varieties such as Granny Smith, Egremont Russet and Braeburn but despite their sharper flavour when eaten raw, they will still produce a delightfully sweet drink.

Makes 400 ml (14 fl oz)

2 carrots

1 apple

2 celery sticks with leaves

150 ml (5 fl oz) ginger ale

Method

Top and tail the carrots and chop into chunks. Twist the stalk off the apple and quarter. Cut the celery into short lengths.

Juice the carrots, apple and celery and add the ginger ale. Pour into glasses and serve at once.

gooseberry buzz

As with so many of the fruit and vegetables we take for granted today, we have Christopher Columbus to thank for bringing peppers back to Europe from the Americas. All peppers start life green, gradually turning red as they ripen, and although green ones have less vitamin C than red, weight for weight they still contain twice as much as an orange. Green peppers are very refreshing in a juice and combined with grapes as they are here, they add a touch of sweetness that contrasts well with the tanginess of gooseberries.

Makes 200 ml (7 fl oz)

1 green pepper

175 g (6 oz) seedless green grapes

200 g (7 oz) gooseberries

1 Tbsp chopped fresh mint

Method

Cut the pepper into wedges – there is no need to discard the stalk or seeds. Pull the grapes off their stalks.

Juice the pepper, grapes and gooseberries and stir in the mint. Pour into glasses and serve.

hot orange spiced tea

Mid morning and you and your pals are flagging? There's no better pick-me-up than a good cup of tea. This spicy version is made using green tea as not only does green make a refreshing and revitalizing cuppa, it's also rich in cancer-fighting antioxidants. As green tea is lighter than a normal breakfast brew, make it with water that's slightly below boiling so as not to scald the leaves and spoil its delicate flavour. If green tea is not to your taste, you can use any blend you prefer.

Makes 1.2 litres (2 pt)
1 large lemon
1 large orange
850 ml (1½ pt) water
4–5 cloves
1 stick of cinnamon
3 green tea bags
Honey or sugar, to taste
Cinnamon sticks and
orange slices, to serve

Method
Squeeze the juice from the lemon and the orange – you will need about 3 tablespoons lemon juice and 75 ml (3 fl oz) orange juice.

Put the water, cloves and cinnamon in a saucepan and bring to the boil. Remove from the heat, leave to stand for 1 minute, then add the tea bags. Set aside to infuse for 5 minutes.

Remove the tea bags and, if sweetening, stir in honey or sugar to taste. Strain in the lemon and orange juices and reheat gently. Serve with cinnamon sticks and orange slices.

in the pink

Red grapes contain higher levels of antioxidants than green grapes, particularly those that can help cut our risk of heart disease, so they're good news not just for red wine lovers but for juice drinkers as well. Rather than bring them back, Columbus actually took vines with him to plant in the New World and later Spanish and Portuguese travellers to South America did the same. With wine such an important part of the Communion service, vineyards flourished and they still do today – but now for different reasons!

Makes 400 ml (14 fl oz)

115 g (4 oz) seedless red grapes

2 pears

¼ pineapple, weighing about 425 g (15 oz)

150 g (5½ oz) strawberries

Method

De-stalk the grapes, twist the stalks off the pears and cut them into quarters or thick wedges. Peel the pineapple and cut the flesh into chunks. Leave the strawberries whole (but halve any very large ones) with the hulls on.

Juice all the fruits. Pour into glasses and serve.

red berry coolade

A long drink to enjoy on balmy summer evenings when homegrown strawberries and redcurrants are at their juiciest and most fragrant. The purée can be made in advance and kept chilled in the fridge ready to be topped up with sparkling mineral water and served when you and your guests can relax and put your feet up.

Makes 1.2 litres (2 pt) when topped up with sparkling water

450 g (1 lb) strawberries

150 g (5½ oz) redcurrants, plus extra sprigs to serve

1 Tbsp caster sugar, or to taste

600 ml (1 pt) sparkling mineral water

Ice cubes

Mint leaves, to garnish

Method

Halve any large strawberries and strip the redcurrants from their stalks using the prongs of a fork. Put the strawberries and currants in a blender, add the sugar and whiz to make a smooth purée. Pour the purée into a jug.

Fill glasses with ice, pour in the strawberry purée to come half way up the level of the ice and top up with sparkling water. Serve at once garnished with extra redcurrant sprigs and a few mint leaves.

six pack

The humble carrot is a real-life nutritional hero containing more beta-carotene than any other vegetable. One large carrot provides enough beta-carotene for your body to convert into an entire day's dose of vitamin A, essential for healthy eyes and seeing in the dark, as our grandmothers used to tell us. Carrot juice is about the only vegetable juice that is refreshing enough to drink on its own but it also makes a useful addition to mixed vegetable juices, its sweetness helping to mask earthy and bitter flavours.

Makes 350 ml (12 fl oz)

1 apple
1 medium beetroot
½ cucumber
½ yellow pepper
1 celery stick with leaves
1 large carrot
Yellow pepper strips, to garnish

Method

Twist the stalk off the apple and cut into quarters. Cut the beetroot into small wedges. Cut the cucumber into chunks and thickly slice the pepper, leaving in the seeds. Chop the celery into short lengths. Top and tail the carrot and cut into chunks.

Juice the apple and vegetables and pour into glasses. Garnish with strips of yellow pepper.

wake-up call

Guarana is a tall shrub native to the Brazilian rain forest and the seeds from its small red fruit contain a form of caffeine called guaranine. Unlike caffeine, guaranine is slow release so the energy boost you get is much more gradual and just the thing to ease you through the day after a heavy night out. Guarana extract is available from health food shops and you only need add a few drops to a juice. If you can't find it, leave it out – the juice will still be the wake-up call you need.

Makes 500 ml (18 fl oz)

1 mango
1 banana
1 kiwi fruit
2 large oranges
2 passion fruit
1 tsp guarana extract

Method
Cut the unpeeled mango flesh away from the stone. Peel the banana and cut into three or four pieces. Peel the kiwi fruit. Cut the rind off the oranges using a vegetable peeler and chop the flesh. Halve the passion fruit and scoop out the pulp and seeds.

Juice all the fruits except the banana. Pour into a blender, add the banana and guarana extract and liquidize until smooth. Pour into glasses and serve.

The passion fruit pulp and seeds can be juiced with the rest of the fruit or warmed to separate the pulp from the seeds and whisked into the juice.

LIQUID SNACKS ON THE GO

berry zinger

In the last couple of years, foodies have hailed the goji (pronounced 'go-gee') berry as a new 'miracle' food – even calling it 'fruit viagra'. Tasting a bit like a slightly salty cranberry, goji berries contain more vitamin C than oranges, more iron than red meat and more beta-carotene than carrots so, although they're expensive to buy, only a few are needed to give a boost to your juice mix. Available dried in packets, the berries need rehydrating by steaming or soaking in a little boiling water before juicing.

Makes 300 ml (½ pt)

1 banana

2 oranges

175 g (6 oz) strawberries

1 Tbsp dried goji berries, steamed or soaked in boiling water to rehydrate

Method

Peel the banana and cut into three or four pieces. Cut the rind away from the oranges using a vegetable peeler, leaving the pith attached to the flesh, and chop into chunks. Keep the strawberries whole unless very large and leave the hulls on. Drain the goji berries if soaked in water.

Juice all the fruit except the banana. Pour into a blender, add the banana and whiz until smooth. Pour into glasses and serve.

caribbean dream

Not many 'good for you' foods taste as sublime as mangoes, which are an excellent source of vitamins, fibre and powerful antioxidants. In traditional Indian ayurvedic medicine, mangoes are highly prized, the whole tree being used to treat patients – fruit for high blood pressure, bark for diarrhoea and the twigs (which are antiseptic when chewed) to protect teeth and gums from decay. Make this drink either using a juicer and a blender or just a blender.

Makes 500 ml (18 fl oz)

2 bananas

1 medium mango

1 medium pineapple (or 150 ml / 5 fl oz pineapple juice if using blender method)

200 ml (7 fl oz) coconut milk

Pineapple wedges and lime, to garnish

Juice method
Peel the bananas and cut into three or four pieces. Cut the unpeeled mango flesh away from the stone. Peel the pineapple and cut into chunks.

Juice the mango and pineapple together, pour into a blender, add the banana and coconut milk and liquidize until smooth.

Blender method
Liquidize the bananas and peeled mango flesh in a blender with the pineapple juice and coconut milk.

Pour into glasses and serve garnished with pineapple wedges and lime.

green as grass

Wheatgrass has many health benefits as it boosts the immune system, aids digestion and gives you extra energy, but it is an acquired taste. If you find wheatgrass too strong to drink as a neat juice – it can best be described as 'liquidized freshly-mown lawn' – try mixing it with other ingredients to enjoy the benefits but mask its flavour.

Makes 300 ml (½ pt)

150 g (5½ oz) carrots

2 apples

Handful of wheatgrass, weighing about 50 g (2 oz)

Method

Top and tail the carrots and cut into chunks. Remove the stalks from the apples and cut the fruit into quarters. If the blades of wheatgrass are long, snip them into shorter lengths with scissors.

Juice the carrots, apples and wheatgrass together and pour into glasses.

liquid lunch

The small purple berries of the acai (pronounced 'ah-sai-ee') tree, native to the Amazonian rainforest, not only contain draw-dropping amounts of antioxidants but also vitamins, calcium, iron and amino acids, so it's not surprising nutritionists have hailed them a true superfood. The actual berries are hard to track down but health food stores and larger supermarkets sell bottles of the juice, so add a slug of that to the finished drink.

Makes 400 ml (14 fl oz)

2 large oranges
200 g (7 oz) blackcurrants, plus extra sprigs to garnish
1 banana
350 g (12½ oz) pineapple
50 ml (2 fl oz) acai berry juice

Method

Cut the rind off the oranges using a vegetable peeler leaving the pith attached to the flesh. Cut the oranges into chunks. Strip the blackcurrants from their stalks with a fork, peel the banana and cut into three or four pieces. Peel the pineapple and slice or chop.

Juice all the fruit except the banana. Pour into a blender, add the banana and acai berry juice and liquidize until smooth. Pour into glasses and serve garnished with extra blackcurrant sprigs.

on your marks

Best of all the remedies for preventing travel sickness and early morning sickness in pregnant mums, ginger can also help fight a cough and cold when you have to keep going through a busy day and can't disappear off home to your bed. Layer the spinach leaves alternately with the apple, green pepper and celery in the feeder tube of the juicer to extract as much liquid from them as you can.

Makes 350 ml (12 fl oz)

3 apples
115 g (4 oz) spinach leaves
1 green pepper
1 celery stick with leaves
1 cm (⅜ in) piece of root ginger

Method

Remove the stalks from the apples and cut into quarters. Chop any large spinach leaves. Thickly slice the pepper leaving in the seeds. Cut the celery into short lengths and slice the ginger thinly without peeling.

Juice all the ingredients together. Pour into glasses and serve.

orchard harvest

Most quince are still found growing in country gardens but in recent years some larger supermarkets and greengrocers have started to stock them during the autumn months. Although quince turn yellow and give off a pleasant aroma when ripe, they're usually too hard and sharp to eat raw but rather than just using them to add bulk in a pie filling, try juicing them with other orchard fruits as, on the nutritional scale, quince are an excellent source of vitamin C. This juice makes an awful lot of froth so leave it to settle for a few minutes before straining off.

Makes 500 ml (18 fl oz)

3 apples

2 pears

325 g (11½ oz) red-skinned plums

1 medium quince, weighing about 300 g (10½ oz)

A few extra thin slices of apple or pear, to serve

Method

Remove the stalks from the apples, pears, plums and quince. Stone the plums and cut all the fruit into wedges or thick slices.

Juice the fruit and leave to settle for 5–10 minutes to give the froth time to subside. Pour into glasses and serve with apple or pear slices.

papaya power shot

Papayas, or pawpaws as they are known in the Caribbean islands and Central America, vary tremendously in size and shape. Some are quite small and pear-shaped, others oval with pointed ends and there are some giants that can weigh up to several kilos that are long, rounded and the size of vegetable marrows. Green papayas can be ripened successfully in a warm kitchen, especially if placed in a bowl alongside a bunch of bananas.

Makes 400 ml (14 fl oz)

½ papaya weighing about 300 g (10½ oz)

2 apples

1 banana

1 lime

Ice cubes, to serve

Lime slices, to garnish

Method

Scoop the seeds out of the papaya and cut the unpeeled flesh into chunks. Remove the stalks from the apples and quarter the fruit. Peel the banana and cut into three or four pieces. Peel the outer rind from the lime and cut the fruit in half.

Juice the papaya and apples with half the lime. Pour into a blender, add the banana and liquidize until smooth. Taste and squeeze in the rest of the lime juice as needed to get the right balance of flavours. Pour into ice-filled glasses and serve garnished with lime slices.

raspberry rejuvenator

Vividly pink and sweetly perfumed, raspberries are a true taste of summer. The berries are thought to be native to Asia where they have grown since prehistoric times but now they're cultivated in many countries and whilst we're mainly familiar with deep pink berries, yellow, orange and purple varieties are grown in other parts of the world. Raspberries freeze well so this juice, which mixes raspberries with three equally fragrant fruits – pineapple, pear and nectarine – can be enjoyed at any time. If nectarines are out of season, add a banana or half a papaya instead.

Makes 500 ml (18 fl oz)

¼ pineapple, weighing about 350 g (12½ oz)

1 pear

1 nectarine

225 g (8 oz) raspberries, plus extra to garnish

Method

Peel the pineapple and cut the flesh into chunks. Remove the stalk from the pear and cut the fruit into quarters or thick slices. Halve the nectarine and remove the stone.

Juice all the fruits together. Pour into glasses and serve garnished with extra raspberries.

red giant

The dominant flavour of this juice is the warm, earthy taste of beetroot so if you find it overpowering, you can tone it down by using an extra apple and a smaller beetroot. The drink is best served chilled, poured into glasses half-filled with ice cubes or crushed ice.

Makes 400 ml (14 fl oz)

2 apples

150 g (5½ oz) red cabbage

2 celery sticks with leaves

1 beetroot, weighing about 150 g (5½ oz)

Ice and thin apple slices, to garnish

Method

Remove the stalks from the apples and cut into quarters. Shred the red cabbage or cut into wedges small enough to fit down the feeder tube of the juicer. Cut the celery into short lengths and the beetroot into small wedges.

Juice the apples, red cabbage, celery and beetroot. Pour into glasses half-filled with ice cubes or crushed ice and serve garnished with thin apple slices.

sea breeze

The sweetness of clementines and ruby red grapefruit are sharpened with the tang of cranberries in this invigorating juice. As cranberries are such hard berries it's worth buying a box of frozen ones and letting them thaw so they become soft before putting them through the juicer. Cranberries have long been prized for their medicinal qualities. North American Indians washed injuries with the juice and made cranberry poultices to draw the poison from arrow wounds. They also taught the Pilgrim Fathers that eating cranberries prevented scurvy and soon American boats carried barrels of cranberries in the same way the English sailors relied on limes. Modern medicine has proved the ruby red juice helps relieve cystitis, one glass being many times more effective than antibiotics.

Makes 400 ml (14 fl oz)

1 red grapefruit

4 clementines

1 pear

50 g (2 oz) frozen cranberries, thawed

Method

Cut the rind away from the grapefruit using a vegetable peeler, leaving the pith attached to the flesh. Cut into wedges small enough to fit down the feeder tube of the juicer. Peel the clementines, remove the stalk from the pear and cut into quarters or wedges.

Juice all the fruits, pour into glasses and serve.

sunny side up

Adding cherries to a juice is a bit of a labour of love as it's a tedious business removing all those stones. If you don't have a special stoning tool – and who does? – run the blade of a small sharp knife around the middle of each cherry, twist the two halves apart and take out the stone, holding the cherries over a bowl as you do this so you catch any juice that runs out.

Makes 500 ml (18 fl oz)

2 apples
300 g (10½ oz) strawberries
175 g (6 oz) cherries

Method
Remove the stalks from the apples and cut the fruit into quarters. Halve any large strawberries but it's not necessary to remove the hulls. Remove the cherry stalks and stones.

Juice the fruits and pour into glasses. Stir well just before serving as the juice separates when left to stand.

veg out

Despite being very rich in the type of beta-carotene that plays a vital role in stopping cancer cells in their tracks, broccoli is never going to be top of everyone's favourite vegetable list. However, juice the florets with other, sweeter fruit and veg, and broccoli quickly turns into a sustaining drink the whole family will love. Serve this juice in small glasses as it's a powerhouse of flavour.

Makes 400 ml (14 fl oz)

1 large sweet potato

1 apple

200 g (7 oz) carrots

6 spears of tenderstem broccoli or 75 g (2½ oz) small broccoli florets

A few mint leaves, to garnish

Method

Cut the unpeeled sweet potato into chunks. Remove the stalk from the apple and cut into quarters. Top and tail the carrots and cut into chunks.

Juice the sweet potato, apple, carrots and broccoli. Pour into glasses and garnish with a few mint leaves.

wizard juice

This juice is a treat for young Harry Potter fans and a great way to celebrate Hallowe'en. The plant chemicals in pumpkin are also believed to provide a gentle aphrodisiac so there's even something for the grown ups too! When peeling the pumpkin don't discard the seeds, just wash off any fibres attached to them, spread the seeds out on a baking sheet and toast until lightly golden in a warm oven. The toasted seeds make a pleasingly crunchy topping for the juice and also contain useful vitamins, minerals and essential fatty acids.

Makes 300 ml (½ pt)
400 g (14 oz) wedge of pumpkin
2 large oranges
Lightly toasted pumpkin seeds, to serve

Method
Peel the pumpkin and scrape out the seeds and fibres clinging to them. Cut the pumpkin flesh into small pieces or it will be hard to push through the juicer. Cut the rind away from the oranges, leaving the pith attached to the flesh. Cut into chunks.

Juice the pumpkin and oranges together and pour into glasses. Sprinkle a few toasted pumpkin seeds on top and serve at once.

LET'S
CELEBRATE

colada crush

Lime juice gives this drink a slightly sharper, more grown up flavour than the popular non-alcoholic cocktail Virgin Colada and it's a good idea to serve extra lime wedges on the side so drinkers can adjust the taste according to personal preference. Serve in well-chilled glasses or poured over plenty of crushed ice.

Makes 800 ml (1 pt 9 fl oz)

½ pineapple, weighing about 500 g (1 lb 2 oz)

1 lime

400 ml (14 fl oz) canned coconut milk

Crushed ice, to serve

Lime rind and extra lime wedges, to garnish

Method

Peel the pineapple and cut into chunks. Peel the rind away from the lime using a vegetable peeler – save the rind to decorate the finished drinks – and cut in half.

Juice the pineapple with half the lime. Pour into a jug and whisk in the coconut milk. Taste and squeeze in more lime juice as necessary.

Chill glasses or half fill with crushed ice and pour in the drink. Garnish with strips of lime rind and serve with extra lime wedges on the side.

cool down cordial

Sweet, fragrant and the perfect thirst-quencher for a warm summer's day. Serve this cordial on its own in well-chilled tumblers or in tall glasses topped up with sparkling water and plenty of ice. Any type of plum can be used but the English Victoria plum works particularly well, its season coinciding with that of wild blackberries, which grow in profusion along hedgerows in late summer.

Makes 350 ml (12 fl oz)

2 apples, plus extra to garnish

350 g (12½ oz) plums

100 g (3½ oz) blackberries

Method

Twist the stalks off the apples and cut the fruit into quarters. Remove the stalks from the plums, halve and take out the stones.

Juice the apples, plums and blackberries. Pour into glasses and garnish each serving with extra apple cut into julienne (thin) strips.

eastern promise

The weird and wonderful dragon fruit looks like a small, fuchsia-pink rugby ball covered in scales that will sit neatly in the palm of your hand. Cut into it and you're in for a surprise. Depending on which variety your supermarket has in stock at the time, the flesh might be white and opaque with tiny black seeds, or it could be a vivid purple-red and the outer skin could be yellow and not pink at all. The fruit of a climbing cactus that dates from the time of the Aztecs in Peru, dragon fruit now grow all over the world and come in many different guises – strawberry pear, pitahaya and pitaya, are just three of the names it is known by. The melon-like flesh is a rich source of fibre, vitamin C and antioxidants and whilst when eaten by itself dragon fruit is not big on flavour, it is very good for juicing, either on its own or with other tropical fruits.

Makes 500 ml (18fl oz)

1 dragon fruit

450 g (1 lb) watermelon (about ⅓–½ mini watermelon)

175 g (6 oz) wedge of pineapple

Method

Cut the dragon fruit and watermelon into chunks without peeling or removing the seeds. Peel the pineapple and slice or cut into chunks.

Juice all the fruits together, pour into glasses and serve.

jungle juice

Cape gooseberries, those shiny golden berries with their delicate Chinese lantern hoods, have to be nature's prettiest fruit. The berries, whilst a little disappointing when eaten on their own, work well in a juice, and left in their gossamer thin wrappers you have the perfect decoration for a party drink. Star fruit, or carambola as they are known in India, are another pretty fruit. Their crisp, tart flesh is good for juicing and sliced across into five-point stars they can be floated on top of a drink or tucked over the side of a glass.

Makes 500 ml (18 fl oz)

300 g (10½ oz) wedge of pineapple

1 papaya, weighing about 450g (1 lb)

1 star fruit

8 Cape gooseberries

2 Tbsp grenadine

Extra slices of fruit, to garnish

Method

Peel the pineapple and cut into slices or wedges. Halve the papaya, scoop out the seeds and chop the unpeeled flesh into wedges. Slice the star fruit and remove the Cape gooseberries from their 'lanterns'.

Juice all the fruit together and whisk in the grenadine. Pour into glasses and serve garnished with extra slices of pineapple, papaya or star fruit.

mango tango

If your mangoes and melon are very ripe and sweet you may want to sharpen the finished juice with some freshly squeezed lime or lemon juice. Serving the juice over plenty of ice will also take the edge off its sweetness. When buying tropical fruits, the best way to check on their ripeness is to pick them up and smell them. They should feel heavy for their size and have a fragrant perfume – if they smell of nothing, the chances are they'll be bland and tasteless, too.

Makes 500 ml (18 fl oz)

2 mangoes

¼ honeydew melon, weighing about 400 g (14 oz)

2 passion fruit

Method

Cut the mango flesh away from the fibrous centre stone. Cut the melon into chunks without removing the seeds – the melon doesn't need peeling unless the skin is particularly coarse. Halve the passion fruit and scoop out the pulp and seeds.

Juice all the fruits, pour into glasses and serve.

melba cooler

Luscious, golden peaches are one of the wonders of the fruit world and are excellent for juicing. High in beta-carotene, they're good for you too, aiding digestion and helping to protect against heart and lung disease. An under-ripe peach is a pale shadow of the fruit when it's in full bloom and will be disappointingly hard and sour to eat, so only juice peaches that smell sweet and give a little when gently squeezed.

Makes 800 ml (1 pt 9 fl oz) when topped up with soda water

2 peaches

2 oranges

150 g (5½ oz) raspberries

Ice cubes, to serve

300 ml (½ pt) soda water

Method

Cut the peaches in half and remove the stones. Cut the rind away from the oranges using a vegetable peeler, leaving the pith attached to the flesh, and cut into chunks.

Juice the peaches, oranges and raspberries together. Pour into ice-filled glasses so the juice comes half way up the level of the ice and top up with soda water.

moonlighter

Grenadine is a syrup made from pomegranate juice that can be bought in larger supermarkets and off-licences and only a splash is needed to give a drink a pretty pink hue. Rather than stir grenadine into the juice, pour the juice into glasses first and then add the grenadine just before serving so it sinks to the bottom and creates a more eye-catching effect. As grapefruit makes the finished juice quite sharp, the grenadine syrup also adds a touch of sweetness.

Makes 400 ml (14 fl oz)

2 apples

½ grapefruit

1 large orange

½ pineapple, weighting about 375 g (13 oz)

Grenadine, to serve

Shredded orange zest, to garnish

Method

Twist the stalks off the apples and cut into quarters. Cut the rind off the grapefruit and the orange using a vegetable peeler, leaving the pith attached to the flesh, and cut into chunks. Peel the pineapple and slice or chop the flesh.

Juice the fruits and pour into glasses. Add a splash of grenadine to each and serve at once. Garnish with shreds of orange zest.

my thai

Hidden inside a mangosteen's deep purple shell is a delicate, lychee-like fruit divided into sections or 'petals', the largest of which usually contains a seed. No relation of the mango, it thrives in the humid climate of south-east Asia and is very sweet, its flavour having been likened to an irresistible blend of strawberries, peaches and vanilla ice cream. Mangosteens aid digestion and like most tropical fruits are rich in vitamin C.

Makes 500 ml (18 fl oz)

1 mangosteen
14 rambutans (or lychees)
1 stalk of lemon grass
300 g (10½ oz)
wedge of pineapple
1 papaya
1 lime

Method

Cut the mangosteen around the centre, remove the top part of the shell and break away the bottom to remove the fruit. Peel the rambutans and remove the stones. Chop the lemon grass, peel the pineapple and cut into wedges. Remove the seeds from the unpeeled papaya and chop into chunks. Shave the rind from the lime and keep to garnish the drinks.

Juice the mangosteen, rambutans, lemon grass, pineapple, papaya and half the lime. Taste and adjust by adding more lime juice if necessary.

Pour into glasses and garnish with twists of lime rind.

orange blush

Cool and refreshing, this juice can be served straight or poured over ice. If you're having a party, increase the quantities of ingredients in proportion to the number of your guests and serve in glass jugs filled with ice cubes and decorated with apple, strawberry and cucumber slices.

Makes 400 ml (14 fl oz)

1 apple
1 ruby grapefruit
¼ cucumber
1 tangerine or satsuma
175 g (6 oz) strawberries

Method

Remove the stalk from the apple and cut into quarters. Cut the rind off the grapefruit with a vegetable peeler, leaving the pith attached to the flesh, and chop into chunks. Cut the cucumber into thick slices and peel the tangerine or satsuma. Cut any large strawberries in half but it's not necessary to remove the hulls.

Juice all the fruit with the cucumber, pour into glasses and serve.

pineapple spritz

Limes have a much stronger flavour than lemons and can be quite overpowering if you add too much to a drink. Limes also vary considerably in size and the amount of juice they contain, so it's worth adding lime juice gradually when the juice has been made and tasting until you get the balance of flavours just right.

Makes 700ml (1¼ pt) when topped up with sparkling water

½ pineapple, weighing about 500 g (1 lb 2 oz)

½ papaya, weighing about 250 g (9 oz)

Juice of 1 lime

300 ml (½ pt) sparkling mineral water

Pineapple leaves, to garnish

Method

Peel the pineapple and cut the flesh into chunks. Scoop the seeds out of the papaya and cut the unpeeled flesh into chunks.

Juice the pineapple and papaya, pour into a jug and add enough of the lime juice to get the right balance of flavours. Pour into glasses and top up with sparkling water. Garnish with pineapple leaves.

rock 'n' roll

Two favourite fruits – apples and nectarines – are given a spicy kick with the addition of sparkling ginger ale and crunchy pomegranate seeds. If white-fleshed nectarines aren't available, pears, white peaches or yellow-fleshed nectarines could all be used instead.

Makes 900 ml (1½ pt)

3 apples

3 white-fleshed nectarines

Ice cubes, to serve

3 Tbsp pomegranate seeds

450 ml (16 fl oz) ginger ale

Method

Twist the stalks off the apples and cut into quarters. Halve the nectarines and remove the stones. Juice the apples and nectarines.

Fill glasses with ice cubes and pour in the juice to come half way up the ice cubes. Sprinkle over the pomegranate seeds, top up with ginger ale and serve at once.

spiced christmas cup

This spiced fruit cup can be served warm or cold and is just the thing to get you into the festive spirit. Loose-skinned clementines are always a favourite with children as they have the sweetness edge over other members of the orange family and are much easier and less messy for small fingers to peel. If you're entertaining a party, make up larger quantities of the cup and serve it in a punch bowl with extra fruit floated on top.

Makes 500 ml (18 fl oz)

5 clementines

2 figs

3 apples

2 large oranges

50 g (2 oz) frozen cranberries, defrosted

1 cm (⅜ in) piece of root ginger

4 whole cloves and 1 cinnamon stick (if serving warm)

Extra slices of clementine and figs, to serve

Method

Peel the clementines and halve the figs. Twist the stalks off the apples and cut into quarters. Cut the rind away from the oranges, leaving the pith attached to the flesh, and chop into chunks. Slice the ginger thinly without peeling.

Juice the clementines, figs, apples, oranges, cranberries and ginger. If serving warm, pour into a saucepan, add the cloves and cinnamon stick and heat gently to a simmer. If serving cold, pour into glasses. Float slices of clementine and fig on top and serve.

summer night

Known as custard apples in the Caribbean, cherimoyas look exactly like big green pine cones but although their skin appears tough and leathery, it is in fact quite delicate and splits easily to reveal the creamy white flesh studded with shiny brown seeds inside. Unlike many tropical fruits, cherimoyas are low in vitamin C but they are a good source of potassium, which is vital for healthy cells and nerves and for controlling blood pressure.

Makes 500 ml (18 fl oz)

1 mango

2 medium oranges

½ canteloupe melon

2 cherimoyas

Extra melon, to garnish

Method

Cut the unpeeled mango flesh away from the fibrous stone. Cut the rind away from the oranges using a vegetable peeler, leaving the pith attached to the flesh, and cut into chunks. Peel the melon and cut into chunks without discarding the seeds. Peel the cherimoyas and, holding the fruit over the feeder tube of the juicer to catch any drips, pull the soft flesh away from the seeds.

Drop the cherimoya flesh down the feeder tube and juice with the other fruits. Pour into glasses and serve neat or over ice, garnished with extra sticks of melon.

sundowner slushie

Prepare the fruit a couple of hours before you're ready to make the drink so it has time to firm up in the freezer. Children will love this 'ice lolly in a glass' but for grown ups who find it a little too sweet, stir in some extra lemon juice.

Makes 1 litre (1¾ pt)
1 nectarine
1 small banana
250 g (9 oz) strawberries
1 small orange
300 ml (½ pt) freshly squeezed orange juice
Juice of 1 lemon

Method
Halve the nectarine and remove the stone. Peel the banana, hull the strawberries and peel the orange, removing the rind and pith. Cut all the fruit into even-size chunks, spread out on a plate or baking sheet lined with non-stick baking parchment and freeze until firm.

Tip the frozen fruit into a blender, add the orange juice and lemon juice and blend until slushy. Tip into glasses and serve at once.

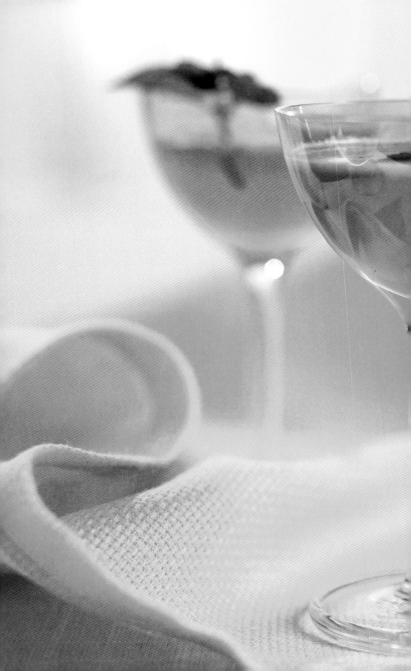

TIME TO
DETOX

bright and breezy

Most of us would agree that juiced on its own cabbage has to be a no-no but because green cabbage helps digestion and stops water retention and constipation, it's about as good as it gets for detoxing – as long as it's harsh flavour can hide behind other, more forgiving, ingredients. In this drink, apple and orange pepper provide sweetness while watercress adds tartness and a vivid shade of green.

Makes 200 ml (7 fl oz)

40 g (1½ oz) watercress

115 g (4 oz) green cabbage

1 apple

1 orange pepper

1 Tbsp chopped fresh parsley

Method

Remove any yellow leaves from the watercress. Roughly chop the cabbage leaves. Twist the stalk off the apple and cut into quarters. Cut the pepper into thick slices without removing the seeds.

Juice the watercress, cabbage, apple and pepper. Stir in the parsley, pour into glasses and serve.

citrus express

Tangy and invigorating with a hint of mint, this blend of citrus fruits really hits the spot when you're feeling a bit sluggish. The juice makes quite a lot of froth so allow it to settle a bit before serving.

Makes 200 ml (7 fl oz)

2 oranges
½ grapefruit
1 lime
6 mint leaves

Method

Cut the rind away from the oranges, grapefruit and lime, leaving the pith attached to the fruit. Chop the oranges and grapefruit into chunks and halve the lime.

Juice the citrus fruits all together. Leave to settle for 5–10 minutes. Cut the mint leaves into thin strips, sprinkle over the juice, pour into glasses and serve.

go green

Since the time of Ancient Greece when Hippocrates built the world's first hospital beside a fresh water stream so he could grow watercress to speed his patients' recovery, the sharp peppery leaves have been recognized as one of nature's great protectors. The Romans believed watercress cured madness – Nero presumably didn't like it! – and its high levels of vitamin C helped prevent scurvy during the Middle Ages. In this detox special, the watercress is blended with spinach, apples and celery, a combination guaranteed to make you feel good.

Makes 300 ml (½ pt)

2 bunches (about 200 g/
7 oz) watercress

100 g (3½ oz) spinach
leaves

2 apples

2 celery sticks,
with leaves

Method
Discard any yellow watercress leaves and shred any large spinach leaves. Twist the stalks off the apples and quarter. Chop the celery.

Juice all the ingredients together in small batches to extract the maximum liquid from the watercress and spinach, keeping a few watercress leaves aside. Pour into glasses and garnish with the reserved sprigs of watercress.

golden girl

Make this juice in early spring when rhubarb is pink and tender rather than later in the season when the stalks become tough, green and more acidic. Orange and ginger are natural partners for rhubarb and adding the sweetness of carrot into the mix, makes this is a refreshing drink. If the juice thickens too much on standing, let it down with mineral water, either still or sparkling.

Makes 400 ml (14 fl oz)

450 g (1 lb) rhubarb
1 large orange
2 medium carrots
1 cm (⅜ in) piece of root ginger
Mineral water, optional

Method
Cut the rhubarb into short lengths, discarding any leaves as these are poisonous. Cut the rind away from the orange, leaving the pith attached to the flesh, and chop into chunks. Top and tail the carrots and cut into chunks. Thinly slice the unpeeled ginger.

Juice the rhubarb, orange, carrots and ginger. Pour into glasses and dilute with mineral water if you find the consistency too thick.

grape harvest

If you feel sluggish in the digestion department, a healthy dose of prunes and pears should sort you out in the nicest possible way. Grapes also help to cleanse the system so this is a great juice for getting you back on track.

Makes 300 ml (½ pt)
4 large pitted prunes
2 pears
115 g (4 oz) seedless red grapes

Method
Soak the prunes in 100 ml (3½ fl oz) boiling water for 1 hour to plump them up. Purée the prunes and their juice in a blender. Remove the stalks from the pears and the grapes and cut the pears into wedges.

Juice the pears and grapes together and whisk or stir in the prune purée, Pour into glasses and serve.

green leaf

The darker green a lettuce the richer it will be in nutrients and, as with spinach and celery, lettuce helps cleanse the body. Sugar snap peas are a good source of iron and the iron is better absorbed into the body if the peas are combined with vitamin C-rich ingredients such as spinach and parsley, as they are in this juice.

Makes 250 ml (9 fl oz)

2 celery sticks with leaves

1 apple

125 g (4½ oz) lettuce, eg Cos

75 g (2½ oz) spinach leaves

75 g (2½ oz) sugar snap peas

Method

Cut the celery into short lengths. Remove the stalk from the apple and cut into quarters. Roughly tear up the lettuce leaves and chop any large spinach leaves.

Juice the celery, apple, lettuce, spinach and sugar snap peas together, pour into glasses and serve.

groovy ruby

The large quantity of refreshing orange juice complements the taste and aroma of the beetroot so you can still benefit from the latter's high vitamin and mineral content even if you don't usually like beetroot on its own as a vegetable. If your beetroot comes with the leaves still attached don't cut these off as they are rich in iron, which boosts blood cells and helps prevent anaemia.

Makes 200 ml (7 fl oz)

1 small beetroot
3 large oranges

Method
Cut the beetroot into small wedges. Cut the rind away from the oranges, leaving the pith attached to the flesh. Chop into chunks and juice the oranges with the beetroot. Pour into glasses and serve.

long and cool

Spinach is one of the best vegetables for detoxing and cucumber is another good system cleanser, as is spirulina, a form of chlorophyll that is one of nature's superfoods. Available as a dense green powder from health food stores, spirulina has a strong flavour that needs balancing with sweeter fruit and vegetables. Mix a little of the juice with the powder, then stir or whisk it back into the remainder. Spirulina is best added to a juice that is already green as it will tint most other coloured juices a less than attractive shade of khaki or sludge green.

Makes 300 ml (½ pt)
115 g (4 oz) spinach leaves
½ cucumber
1 yellow pepper
1 apple
1 tsp spirulina powder
Cucumber ribbons,
to serve

Method
Shred any large spinach leaves.
Cut the cucumber into short lengths.
Thickly slice the yellow pepper without removing the seeds. Remove the stalk from the apple and cut into quarters.

Juice the spinach, cucumber, pepper and apple. Mix a little of the juice with the spirulina powder until smooth and stir or whisk this back into the rest of the juice. Pour into glasses and serve with cucumber ribbons, made by drawing a vegetable peeler down the length of a cucumber and shaving off thin strips.

on the beet

Potatoes aren't normally a vegetable you would eat raw but they work well in a juice, being rich in potassium, vitamin C, calcium and other nutrients that help combat heart and lung diseases. Radishes have similarly healthy credentials and beetroot is well known for its ability to flush out the system. Add in the digestive benefits of carrots and you have a mighty juice that packs a punch.

Makes 250 ml (9 fl oz)

1 small beetroot

200 g (7 oz) carrots, plus extra julienne strips to garnish

1 potato, weighing about 225 g (8 oz)

4 radishes

Method

Cut the beetroot into small wedges. Top and tail the carrots and chop into chunks. Cut the unpeeled potato into chunks that will fit down the feeder tube of the juicer. Top and tail the radishes.

Juice all the vegetables together, pour into glasses and serve garnished with julienne strips of carrot.

pepper plus

Fibre from the red pepper and the carrot will help keep your digestive system running smoothly, whilst the cleansing effect of orange is almost guaranteed to make you feel better. The vegetables add a touch of sweetness, which balances the spiky citrus kick of the orange.

Makes 200 ml (7 fl oz)
1 red pepper
1 medium carrot
1 medium orange

Method
Thickly slice the pepper without removing the seeds. Top and tail the carrot and slice into chunks. Cut the rind away from the orange using a vegetable peeler, leaving the pith attached to the flesh, and chop.

Juice the pepper, carrot and orange together, pour into glasses and serve.

prune blast

Choose sweet, juicy prunes such as the French pruneaux d'Agen and soak them for 10-15 minutes in warm water to plump them up before juicing. Prunes are excellent for cleansing the system, carrots add fibre, celery is a natural diuretic and the peach adds its own special fragrance to the juice.

Makes 300 ml (½ pt)
4 large pitted prunes
1 peach
2 celery sticks with leaves
2 medium carrots

Method
Soak the prunes in 100 ml (3½ fl oz) boiling water for 1 hour. Purée the prunes with their soaking water in a blender. Halve the peach and remove the stone. Chop the celery into short lengths. Top and tail the carrots and cut into chunks.

Juice the peach, celery and carrots together and whisk or stir in the prune purée. Pour into glasses and serve.

spring clean

This juice is quite sweet as the carrots and celery mask most of the earthiness of the beetroot. If you're a beetroot lover, replace one of the carrots or sticks of celery with another small beetroot.

Makes 200 ml (7 fl oz)

2 medium carrots

¼ cucumber, weighing about 125 g (4½ oz)

1 small beetroot, weighing about 75 g (2½ oz)

2 celery sticks with leaves

Crushed ice

Small dill sprigs, to garnish

Method

Top and tail the carrots and chop into chunks. Cut the cucumber into short lengths. Cut the beetroot into small wedges. Chop the celery into short lengths.

Juice all the vegetables together. Serve poured over crushed ice and garnish with a few small sprigs of dill.

think pink

Another newcomer to the super-fruit league is noni, an oblong yellow-green fruit dotted with brown spots. Originally from south east Asia, where it's been around for 2,000 years, it now thrives in tropical places all over the world such as Tahiti, Hawaii, Australia and the Caribbean, where it is known as the 'pain-killer tree'. Noni juice is reputed to help you stay younger for longer and promotes a feeling of general well-being by helping to cleanse and purify the system. Bottles of noni juice are available from health food shops and although expensive, a little goes a long way.

Makes 300 ml (½ pt)

450 g (1 lb) wedge of watermelon
50 g (2 oz) redcurrants
75 g (2½ oz) strawberries
1 Tbsp noni juice
Mint leaves, to garnish

Method

Cut the watermelon into chunks without removing the skin or seeds. Pull the redcurrants from their stalks. Halve any large strawberries – it's not necessary to hull them.

Juice the fruit all together and stir or whisk in the noni juice. Pour into glasses and serve garnished with a few mint leaves.

true blue

They might be regarded as the redcurrant's poor relation but small, tangy blackcurrants with their almost musky fragrance are delicious in a juice, adding a sharp, distinctive flavour. The small black bead-like currants contain far higher quantities of vitamin C than citrus fruits such as lemons and they freeze well so, if you grow your own, any surplus can be frozen and juiced later to ward off winter colds.

Makes 200 ml (7 fl oz)

1 apple
75 g (2½ oz) blackcurrants
75 g (2½ oz) blueberries
75 g (2½ oz) blackberries
Ice cubes

Method
Remove the stalk from the apple and cut into quarters. Pull the blackcurrants off their stalks.

Juice all the fruits together, pour into glasses and serve over ice.

watercress cooler

Nashi pears, or Asian pears as they are also known, look like a rough, brown-skinned apple and have an apple's crunch but the perfumed fragrance of a pear. High in fibre and vitamin C they juice well and, by combining them with melon and watercress, they have a cleansing effect on the system, the watercress giving a slightly sharp edge to the sweet nashi pears and melon.

Makes 400 ml (14 fl oz)

2 nashi pears

200 g (7 oz) wedge of Galia or Ogen melon

75 g (2½ oz) watercress

Method

Remove the stalks from the nashi pears and cut into quarters or wedges. Peel the melon if the skin is hard and cut the flesh into chunks without removing the seeds. Pick any yellow leaves off the watercress.

Juice the pears, melon and watercress together, pour into glasses and serve.

index

acai berry juice 108
Agent orange 74
apples 16, 18, 24, 32, 52, 60, 86, 96, 106, 110, 112, 114, 118, 122, 124, 132, 142, 146, 150, 152, 160, 164, 170, 174, 186
Apricot and orange spritz 76
apricots 26, 50, 76

Back to your roots 78
bananas 16, 24, 54, 98, 102, 104, 114, 156
beetroot 42, 96, 118, 172, 176, 182
Berry nice 46
Berry zinger 102
blackberries 34, 46, 80, 132, 186
blackcurrants 108, 186
Blue moon 80
blueberries 24, 34, 46, 80, 186
Breakfast smoothie 16
Bright and breezy 160
Bright eyes 18
broccoli 124

cabbage 62, 160
    red 66, 118
Cape gooseberries 136
Caribbean dream 104
carrots 18, 36, 42, 56, 66, 78, 86, 96, 106, 124, 166, 176, 178, 180, 182
celery 36, 56, 74, 86, 96, 110, 118, 164, 170, 180, 182
cherimoyas 154
cherries 122
Chill out 48
Chill out lemon 82
Citrus blitz 20
Citrus express 162
clementines 120, 152
coconut milk 104, 130
Colada crush 130

Cool down cordial 132
cranberries 24, 120, 152
cucumber 32, 56, 78, 96, 146, 174, 182

dandelion leaves 84
dragon fruit 134

Eastern promise 134

fennel 84
figs 54, 152
Fine and dandy 84
Four-all 22
Fruit-full 24

ginger ale 86, 150
Ginger fizz 86
ginger, root 42, 110, 152, 166
Go green 164
goji berries, dried 102
Golden girl 166
Golden glow 50
gooseberries 88
Gooseberry buzz 88
Grape harvest 168
grapefruit 20, 38, 142, 162
  red 120
grapes 52
  green 88
  red 92, 168
Green as grass 106
Green leaf 170
Green light 54
grenadine 136, 142
Groovy ruby 172
guarana extract 98
Guava buzz 26
guavas 26

Hot orange spiced tea 90

In the mood 54
In the pink 92

Jungle juice 136
Just peachy 28
Just relax 56

kiwi fruit 16, 32, 40, 52, 98

lemons 58, 60, 68, 76, 82, 90, 156
lettuce 170
limes 20, 114, 130, 144, 148, 162
Liquid lunch 108
Long and cool 174
lychees 64, 144

mandarins 28
Mango tango 138
mangoes 50, 98, 104, 138, 154
mangosteen 144
Melba cooler 140
melon, cantaloupe 54, 58, 154
  Galia 34, 188
  honeydew 64, 80, 138
  Ogen 34, 58, 188
Melon breeze 58
Moonlighter 142
Morning glory 30
My Thai 144

nashi pears 188
nectarines 22, 116, 150, 156
Night cap 60
No stress 62
noni juice 184

On the beet 176
On your marks 110
Orange blush 146
oranges 16, 18, 20, 40, 50, 54, 60, 74,

76, 90, 98, 102, 108, 126, 140, 142,
152, 154, 156, 162, 166, 172, 178
Orchard harvest 112

papaya 38, 70, 74, 114, 136, 144, 148
Papaya power shot 114
parsley 18, 160
parsnips 62, 78
passion fruit 34, 40, 70, 98, 138
peaches 28, 50, 140, 180
pears 22, 26, 48, 66, 92, 112, 116, 120, 168
Pepper plus 178
peppers, green 88, 110
  orange 160
  red 178
  yellow 84, 96, 174
pineapple 56, 70, 92, 104, 108, 116,
  130, 134, 136, 142, 144, 148
Pineapple spritz 148
Pink panther 64
plums 30, 116, 132
pomegranate seeds 28, 52, 150
pomelo 30
potato 176
Power punch 32
Prune blast 180
prunes 168, 180
pumpkin 126
Purple haze 34

quince 112

radishes 176
rambutans 144
raspberries 30, 46, 64, 116, 140
Raspberry rejuvenator 116
Red alert 36
Red berry coolade 94
Red giant 118
Red mist 66
redcurrants 94, 184

rhubarb 166
Rock 'n' roll 150
Rosy glow 38

satsumas 146
Sea breeze 120
Six pack 96
Spiced Christmas cup 152
spinach 32, 48, 84, 110, 164, 170, 174
spirulina powder 174
Spring clean 182
Start right 40
strawberries 22, 24, 38, 46, 64, 92,
  94, 102, 122, 146, 156, 184
sugar snap peas 170
Summer night 154
Summer special 68
Sundown slushie 156
Sunny side up 122
sweet potato 62, 78, 124

tangerines 146
tea, China 68
  green 90
Think pink 184
tomatoes 36
Tropical teaser 70
True blue 186

Up-beet 42

Veg out 124

Wake-up call 98
watercress 42, 48, 160, 164, 188
Watercress cooler 188
watermelon 58, 134, 184
wheat germ 24
wheatgrass 106
Wizard juice 126